LOOK

I'm a Scientist

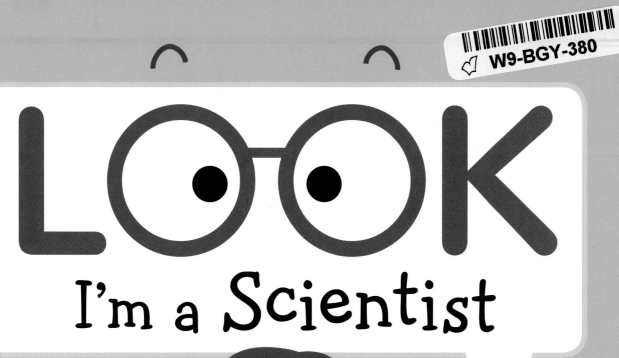

DK

For the grown-ups

This book is full of hands-on activities that will tap straight into your child's natural scientific curiosity. Each activity is designed to let your child play and learn with all their senses. Together, you can grow their love of science and their understanding of the world.

Here are a few tips to help you along the way:

Your child should be supervised at all times when conducting these experiments, but try to give them time and space to lead the direction of play. The questions in this book are suggestions. Let your child ask, and answer, their own questions.

•

Involve your child in the preparation of each activity. Let them measure, mix, and follow the instructions. The measurements in this book are often proportional, so you can use the same cup or mug to measure equal quantities of ingredients.

•

Adult Alert stars show where your child will need extra grown-up help.

•

Protect the area where your child will be playing and encourage them to wear old clothes. Be especially careful when using food coloring, which can mark fabrics and temporarily stain skin. Being prepared lets your child enjoy themselves to their fullest. Making a mess is part of fun and learning!

Adult ALERT!

DK | Penguin Random House

Editor Hélène Hilton
Design and Illustration Rachael Parfitt Hunt
US Senior Editor Shannon Beatty
Additional Design and Illustration Charlotte Milner
Educational Consultant Penny Coltman
Photographer Dave King
Additional Photography Lol Johnson
Jacket Designer Charlotte Milner
Jacket Co-ordinator Francesca Young
Editorial Assistance James Mitchem, Marta Rybarczyk
Design Assistance Eleanor Bates, Rachael Hare, Pauline Korp
Pre-production Dragana Puvacic
Production Amy Knight
Managing Editor Penny Smith
Managing Art Editors Mabel Chan, Gemma Glover
Publisher Mary Ling
Creative Director Jane Bull

First American Edition, 2017
Published in the United States by DK Publishing
345 Hudson Street, New York, New York 10014

A catalog record for this book is available from the Library of Congress.
ISBN: 978-1-4654-7480-3

DK books are available at special discounts when purchased in bulk for sales promotions, premiums, fund-raising, or educational use. For details, contact: DK Publishing Special Markets, 345 Hudson Street, New York, New York 10014 SpecialSales@dk.com

Printed and bound in China

The publisher would like to thank the following for their kind permission to reproduce their photographs:
(Key: a-above; b-below/bottom; c-center; f-far; l-left; r-right; t-top)
43 Dorling Kindersley: Natural History Museum, London (br). **44-45 Getty Images:** Navaswan (t).
45 Getty Images: Darren Pearson (dariustwin) (cr). All other images © Dorling Kindersley
For further information see: www.dkimages.com

And a big thank you to all the little scientists who acted as models –
Abigail Blake, Hannah Blake, Ella Chen, Harleen De Vera, Betty Johnson,
Ella Johnson, Lola Johnson, Elijah Knight, Eli May Piene-Halpin,
Lucas Robson, Sofia Schwarts, and Elliot Tannazi.

A WORLD OF IDEAS:
SEE ALL THERE IS TO KNOW
www.dk.com

Contents

Little brains have big ideas!

You don't need a **white coat**, **safety goggles**, and a **fancy lab** to be a scientist. You already have everything you need to be the best scientist ever: **your brain** and **your amazing senses**!

Curious questions

Science is about asking questions, as much as answering them. Here are some questions to ask yourself as you play.

- What will happen if I do this?

- What can I hear, smell, see, taste, and feel?

- Why did that happen?

- Does the same thing always happen?

- How can I find out more?

Your science senses

Brain
Your brain is not one of your senses, but it gathers information from them all and tries to understand it.

Hearing
There are so many noises to listen to! What can you hear?

Sight
Super scientists use their eyes for looking really, really carefully.

Smell
Use your nose to find smelly clues!

Taste
Your tongue is great at tasting different flavors.

Touch
Your skin tells you how things feel. Be careful with objects that might be hot, cold, sharp, or that might hurt.

Let's see what we can do!

Ooey gooey slime

Mix up your own super-easy **slime**. Then see how it acts as both a **liquid** and a **solid**.

You will need:

2 cups cornstarch

+

1 to 2 cups dishwashing liquid

+

food coloring

+

1 to 2 cups warm water

Scientists say that slime is "viscous." That means it's thick and sticky.

1

In a bowl, **mix** the cornstarch, dishwashing liquid, and a few drops of food coloring.

2

Add a little of the **water** to your slime and mix until **smooth**.

pour

mix

smooth

3

Keep adding **water** and mix until your slime is **runny** but **thick**.

Time to get all slimy! Ewwwww!

Experiment to see how much water, dishwashing liquid, and cornstarch makes the perfect slime.

slimy

Now turn your slime into aliens!

Let it flow

Hold the slime in your hands to watch it **flow** through your fingers like a **liquid**.

squash and squeeze

Roll it

If you roll up the slime, the tiny pieces of cornstarch inside squash together and the slime becomes **hard** like a **solid**.

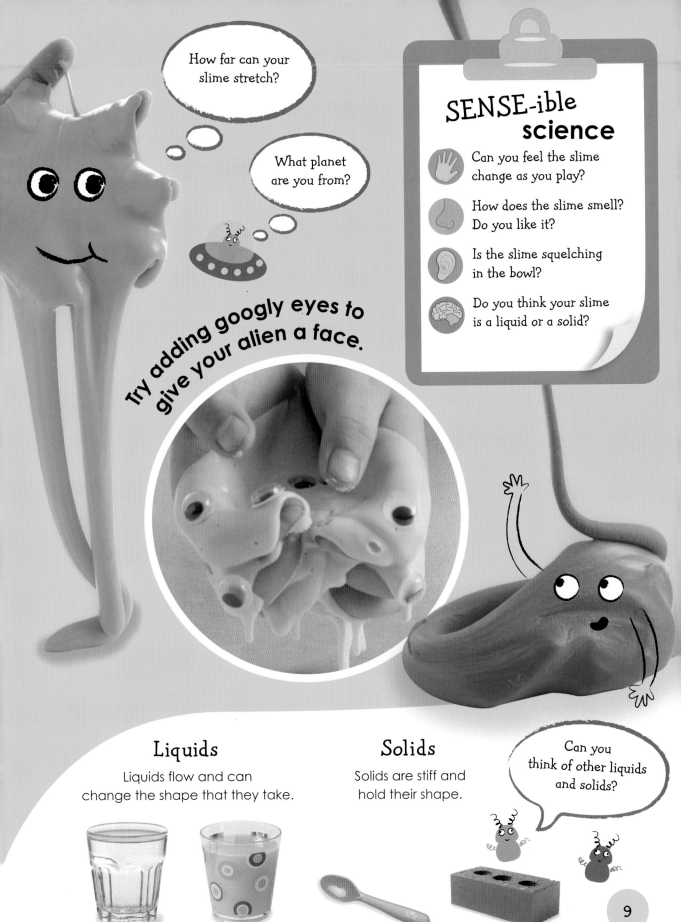

How far can your slime stretch?

What planet are you from?

Try adding googly eyes to give your alien a face.

SENSE-ible science

Can you feel the slime change as you play?

How does the slime smell? Do you like it?

Is the slime squelching in the bowl?

Do you think your slime is a liquid or a solid?

Liquids

Liquids flow and can change the shape that they take.

water

juice

Solids

Solids are stiff and hold their shape.

spoon

brick

Can you think of other liquids and solids?

9

Iceberg animal rescue

Water is a **liquid**, but what happens when it gets very cold? It freezes into **ice**—a **solid**! Make an **iceberg** then **melt the ice** to rescue the animals.

You will need:

plastic tub

plastic toy animals

water

blue food coloring

Water flows. It feels wet and you can splash in it! Where can you see water around you?

10

Icebergs are huge blocks of ice that float in the sea.

Pour **water** and a few drops of food coloring in a freezable tub. Add your **animals**.

I use my flippers to swim.

Yay! It's my turn next!

Can you splash?

We're having a pool party!

It's getting a bit crowded!

2

Put the tub and your toy animals in the **freezer** overnight.

3

Is the iceberg frozen? Turn the tub upside down until your iceberg pops out.

Adult ALERT!

Check your freezer to see what is happening to the water. When it gets to 32°F (0°C), the water will start to freeze.

Brrr! It's cold in the freezer.

To the **rescue!**

water
Warm water heats up the ice and melts it.

sponge
Use a sponge to soak up the water.

salt
Salt turns solid ice back into liquid water.

spoon and fork
Carefully use a spoon or fork to break the ice.

Squeeze
Pour **warm** water on the ice or squeeze it on with a sponge.

I'm free!

Melting the ice

Scatter some **salt** on the iceberg to see what happens! Does it **melt** the ice?

In real life, penguins and polar bears never meet. They live on opposite sides of the world.

Thanks for rescuing us!

Spoon rescue

Carefully use a spoon or fork to **wiggle** the animals free.

melting

From ice to water

If water gets cold enough, the molecules (the tiny water pieces) hook to one another and stop moving. The water goes stiff and turns to ice (it freezes from a liquid to a solid). Melting is the opposite of freezing.

solid ice

liquid water

SENSE-ible science

What is the best way to melt the ice?

Does the ice make a cracking sound?

Can you see the ice melting back to liquid water?

Can you feel the difference between the ice and water?

Float your iceberg in warm water to watch it melt super fast.

The warmth from your hands makes the ice melt. The ice makes your hands cold too.

How does your iceberg feel?

Brrr!

Blowing in the wind

Air is all around you. When air moves from one place to another, we call it **wind**. You can't see air, but it's **strong** enough to blow your hat off!

Attaching the screw eyes can be tricky. Ask an adult for help.

Adult ALERT!

Hear the wind

You can make simple **wind chimes** with sticks. Hang them outside then listen to the wind **bang** the sticks together.

You breathe in and breathe out air with your lungs. You can use this air to blow on a paper pinwheel and make it spin.

string

stick

screw eye

paint to decorate

SENSE-ible science

How does the wind feel in your hair?

Does the wind smell like anything?

Can you think of ways that wind is useful?

embroidery hoop or coat hanger

See the wind

Make this rainbow **wind catcher**, then watch the wind move the ribbons. Thread ribbons onto a hoop and hold it up outside. The wind will **lift the ribbons** like a kite. Can you see which way the wind is blowing?

Fun with balloons

Balloons are great to **play** and **experiment** with. Take **a big breath in** and blow into your balloon to fill it with **air**. Then try these tricks.

Hair-raising electricity

Rub the balloon on your hair. Then lift the balloon above your **head**. What happens to your **hair**?

It's electric!

Rubbing the balloon on your hair makes a special kind of electricity called *static electricity*. This makes your hair stick to the balloon.

I'm powered by electricity.

Balloon **rocket**

Thread the string through a drinking straw.

tape

Tie up the string tightly.

Thread string through a straw and tie it up tightly. Blow up your balloon, pinching the end closed. Tape it to the straw.
Ready, set... let go!

balloon

When you let go, air rushes out of the balloon and pushes the balloon forward. How fast will it go?

Make a hovercraft

Stick a pop-up bottle cap onto an old CD or DVD. Pull a blown-up balloon on top. Then open the cap. Push your **hovercraft to watch it glide** along the table!

Air flows out of the balloon and through the cap. This makes an air cushion under the disc and lifts the hovercraft a tiny bit off the table.

19

Tiny bubbles

You can make **great bubbles** by trapping **air** inside **soapy water**. These bubbles are small and super soft.

You will need:

These bubbles are so tiny that you have to look closely to see them. Together they make a thick foam.

Pour

+ warm water
+ soap
+ food coloring

1

Very carefully, **grate the soap** into little pieces. Be careful of your fingers!

Adult ALERT!

cheese grater

2

Add the grated soap to warm water and mix it around until it **dissolves**.

20

3

Whizz up bubbles in your mixture with a hand mixer until it makes a thick foam that holds its shape.

soft and squishy

Adult ALERT!

hand mixer

plastic tub

4

Add food coloring to make your bubbles **more colorful**.

What **shapes** can you make?

What shape is a bubble?

Play with your bubbles, but DON'T EAT THEM!

BIG bubbles

Use a Hula-Hoop to make these **HUGE** bubbles!
How tall can you make them?

You will need:

inflatable pool
half-full of water

+

1 bottle of
dishwashing liquid

+

Glycerine only works if
you make your bubble mix
a few days ahead.

1 bottle of
glycerine (optional)

How *big* is your *bubble?*

Glycerine makes
bubbles stronger.

Mix all your ingredients in an inflatable **pool**. Dip a **Hula-Hoop** into the mix and **slowly lift it** out to make a long bubble.

Hula-Hoop

SENSE-ible science

What bubble shapes can you make?

Can you see colors in your big bubbles?

Do the big bubbles feel the same as the tiny bubbles?

What other objects could you use as a bubble wand?

Hear that sound?

SENSE-ible science

Do all noises sound the same?

Can you see the water rippling when you tap the bottles?

What different sounds can you make?

When objects **touch** each other, they **vibrate** (move backward and forward). This makes the **air** vibrate, too. Your ears pick up the **vibrations** and **your brain turns them into sounds**

Musical bottles

Fill glass bottles with water. When you **tap** the bottles, the water and the air inside them **vibrate**. Depending on how much water and air they contain, the bottles make **different sounds**.

wooden spoon

tap tap

Spin the drum so that the beads hit the paper plates and make a banging sound.

beads

paper plate

Spinning drum

To make a drum, tape a wooden **spoon** between 2 **paper plates**. Stick the plates together. Then attach 2 **beads** to the sides of the plates with **string**.

string

wooden spoon

glass bottles

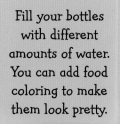

Fill your bottles with different amounts of water. You can add food coloring to make them look pretty.

Can you make a tune? Try tapping different parts of the bottles to see if it sounds the same.

Let's make a potion

Be a **science wizard** with this awesome potion experiment. This is a real **chemical reaction** you can do at home. It's messy, so be prepared!

You will need:

vinegar + dishwashing liquid + food coloring

Trial and error is a big part of being a scientist. Try this experiment with different amounts of the ingredients to see if anything changes.

glitter and glitter stars

Make your potion magical!

baking soda

1

Half fill a glass jar with **vinegar** and squeeze in a little **dishwashing liquid**.

The dishwashing liquid will help make it ...

dishwashing liquid

really, really bubbly!

2

Add a few drops of food coloring and some glitter. Give the mixture a **good stir**.

Wow!
Pretty glitter stars!

3

Add a big spoonful of **baking soda** and **stir** it in. Quickly take out the spoon and **watch what happens.**

Watch your potion...

Fizzy chemistry

When vinegar and baking soda meet, they react with each other. Together, they make a gas called carbon dioxide. This gas floats away so it makes lots of bubbles as it escapes.

fizz!

The Milky Way

Make these awesome milky **planets** and watch the colors **swirl** around and around as the **milk** tries to escape from the dish**washing liquid**.

You will need:

whole milk + dishwashing liquid + cotton swabs + food coloring

1 Pour **milk** into a dish or jar lid and add a few drops of **food coloring**.

2 Dip a cotton swab in **dishwashing liquid**. Swirl the cotton swab around in the milk and watch what happens.

SENSE-ible science

- What happens when the colors mix?
- Do you know the names of any planets?
- Do your milky planets look like real planets?

Our galaxy

At night, our galaxy looks like a white starry path, so we call it the **Milky Way**.

Real planets have swirls too. These are usually huge storm clouds.

Swirling milk

The dishwashing liquid makes the fat inside the milk move around in all directions. By adding color, you can see the milk swirl and twirl.

Homemade playdough

Playdough is even **better** when you make it yourself! **Mix** your ingredients together to make a really squishable dough.

You will need:

food coloring (optional)

2 cups flour

+

1 cup salt

+

2 tablespoons of oil

+

2 teaspoons of cream of tartar

+

2 cups water

water

cream of tartar

salt

oil

flour

1

Pour **all the ingredients** (except the food coloring) into a saucepan.

2

mix mix mix

Place the pan on a **medium heat.** Mix everything together until the ingredients form a **dough.**

Adult ALERT!

Make your dough colorful!

squeeze

Be careful, it's hot!

3

Let your dough cool, then add food coloring. Now **squeeze** the dough until it's **smooth and soft.**

Play with your **playdough**

Your printing tool kit:

rolling pin   leaves, pinecones, and flowers   cutters

Make your dough any color.

ROAR!

Look at all the colors!

Prints and shapes

Roll your playdough flat with a rolling pin. Then use objects to make really **bumpy** prints or **cut out** fun shapes.

SENSE-ible science

What objects can you print in your playdough?

Does your playdough smell like anything?

What prints can you see most clearly?

Can you describe how your playdough feels?

It's like a rainbow!

Let it snow!

Snow is made when **tiny ice crystals** inside clouds stick together and become a snowflake. You can make **pretend snow**, then build your very own **snowman**!

You will need:

We used to be snowflakes!

2 cups baking soda

Most rain starts off as snow. But it melts before it gets to the ground and turns into raindrops.

2 cups shaving cream

1

Mix the ingredients with your hands. Your snow should be **crumbly** but **stick together** if you pat it together into a **snowball**.

Can you make a snowball?

Mix it!

2

If the mixture is **too crumbly**, add more shaving cream. If it's **too wet**, add more baking soda.

Now you can make me and some friends to chill with!

Sprinkle your soft snow.

It's snowing!

Now make a snowy person.

3

Roll 2 snowballs to make your snowman's **body** and **head**. Try adding googly eyes to decorate.

Hi! Nice to meet you.

38

SENSE-ible science

 Does your snow feel like real snow?

 Can you hear your snow squelching?

 Have you ever seen real snow?

> This hat and scarf will keep me warm and cozy. Thanks!

39

Be a tabletop scientist

There's lots of **fun and easy science** you can do while you're waiting for your dinner. These 3 tabletop experiments play with **light** to **trick your eyes.**

Which way is the ladybug facing?

The ladybug trick

Draw a picture on a piece of paper and hold it **behind a glass of water**. Slowly move the glass toward you. Look through the glass to see the ladybug **turn around**.

For this trick to work, your drawing has to be facing either left or right, but not straight ahead.

What can you see inside the spoon?

Choose your shiniest spoon for this experiment.

Does the water really break the straw?

Take it out of the water to find out.

Mirror spoon

Look at your reflection in a **shiny spoon.** Then turn the spoon over. The **curve** of the spoon changes your reflection! Which side makes your face turn **upside-down?**

Silly straw

Put a **straw** into a glass of water and look at it **through the side.** Does the straw **look broken?**

When tiny things get big

Magnifying glasses help scientists look at things **very**, **very** closely. Try it! You might **see** things you'd **never noticed** before.

How does it work?

When you get closer to things, you can see them in **more detail**. But if you look at something too closely, it will look **blurry**. Magnifying glasses have a **curved lens** that makes things look **closer**, without making them blurry.

Try it yourself! Grab a magnifying glass and look at things on this page and around you. It's your turn to be a scientific observer.

Play with clouds

Clouds can be **fluffy**, **puffy**, or **wispy**, but they all have one thing in common. They are made of water.

Cloud painting

Place a mirror on the ground outside. Can you see the clouds in the mirror? Use a paintbrush and shaving cream to color them in.

Are you painting me?

paintbrush

mirror

shaving cream

44

Clouds are made up of tiny droplets of water. When the droplets fall, they become rain. What do you think clouds would feel like to touch?

What are rainbows?

When sunlight shines through raindrops, the raindrops split the light into lots of colors. This makes a rainbow.

Cloud spotting

When you're outside, look up at the sky. What shapes can you spot among the clouds?

That cloud looks like a rabbit!

Look, you're a scientist!

Lots of scientists follow the same rules when they discover something new. You can follow them, too. Think about the experiments you have done. Can you follow **the scientific method?**

1. What is this?

When scientists observe something interesting, they come up with a question about it, to find out more. **Scientists call this question a "hypothesis."**

2. What will happen?

Before trying out their hypothesis, scientists try to guess what the answer will be. **Scientists call this a "prediction."**

3. Time to play

Scientists love to play. They test their ideas to try them out. Sometimes it goes wrong and they try to fix it. **Scientists call this an "experiment."**

A scientist's work is never done. There's always more to ask, more to discover, and more fun to be had!

4. What does it all mean?

Scientists think about what happened in their experiment and what they can learn from it. **Did you predict what would happen? Was it a surprise?**

Good job!

....

is a scientist!

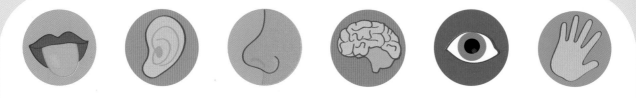

Index